Eyre Square 300: Aspects of its History

Published by: Brendan McGowan, 19 Woodview Court, Killala, Co. Mayo, Ireland

Email: takingtheboat@hotmail.com

Text Copyright: © Brendan McGowan 2012

Design, Layout & Typesetting: Barry Jordan at Spear Design www.speardesign.ie

Printing & Reprographics: CastlePrint, Galway.

ISBN: 978-0-9563757-2-8

Left: Eyre Square, Galway (c. 1870-1910). Courtesy of the National Library of Ireland.

Front Cover Image: Fahy and Gilmore children with Sean Phàdraic (c. 1971). Courtesy of Teresa Gilmore.

Back Cover Image: Eyre Square, Galway (c. 1870-1910). Courtesy of National Library of Ireland.

Eyre Square

300

Aspects of its History
Brendan McGowan

Left: John Hinde postcard of Eyre Square (c. 1970).
Author's Collection.

Below: Valentine's postcard of 'Ancient Gateway,
Galway' (c. 1940s). Author's Collection.

Contents

Foreword
Ronnie O'Gorman

On May 12 1712, Edward Eyre, whose forebears came to Galway with Cromwell some 60 years earlier, gifted a plot of land outside the town's walls, east of the main gate at William Street, to Galway Corporation. Three hundred years later that piece of ground which still bears his name is at the heart of a busy city.

Through the three centuries that piece of ground kept re-inventing itself until it emerged as the popular 'square' that it is today. Shortly after the 1798 rebellion General Meyrick, who had been sent to Ireland to put down any further unrest, impressed the population of the town as he put his Redcoats through their paces up and down the green, as it was then known.

As the town expanded handsome houses appeared around its edge; and when soldiers were not on parade, it became a busy and noisy market place teeming with farmers selling their animals and vegetables.

In the early 1800s it became the Galway terminus for the Bianconi horse-drawn cars, known as 'Bians', the only form of public transport at the time. When the railway came in the 1850s the green was crowned with the imposing Midland Great Western Railway Hotel (now the Meyrick). It was here that the well known novelist Edith Somerville 'breakfasted leisurely ... serenaded by the screams of pigs.'

Its famous railings were erected in 1842 giving the city council some control as to its usage, and who should be allowed to go in and out of its gates. The unanimous opinion of the council was, however, that it should be open 'to all decently clad people who chose to walk in it'. The green, now became a respectable place; and acquired a more suitable name, that of a 'square', although it's not quite a square in measurement.

The square became a venue for all sorts of public events, such as funfairs and political meetings. The Liberator Daniel O'Connell and Charles Stewart Parnell addressed crowds there. More poignantly, it was the base for British Army recruitment drives during the Great War 1914; and where victory fires were lit following the armistice, four years later. By contrast during World War II it was used as a vast turf depot, to replace the absence of British coal.

Through the centuries it has also gained several monuments reflecting important historical and cultural events.

With its flowerbeds and young trees today Eyre Square is criss-crossed by thousands of people coming and going; and in fine weather it is a magnet for office and shop workers who throw off as much clothes as is decent, and soak up the sun as they eat their lunch. No one seems to mind. Eyre Square is very much a people's space.

Galway is a city full of stories. In this beautifully presented, and well researched book, Brendan McGowan tells the story of our square very well indeed. He reminds us of the importance of heritage and pride of place, and make me conscious that we are missing two important and popular monuments: the Crimean cannons, and the popular Pádraic Ó Conaire statue. I hope they will soon be returned to their rightful place.

Eyre Square 300: Aspects of its History is a welcome addition to our growing Galway Library.

Ronnie O'Gorman, *Galway Advertiser*

Left: Aerial view of Eyre Square (1984).
© RTÉ Stills Library.

Introduction
Brendan McGowan

On 12 May 1712, Edward Eyre, Mayor of Galway, gifted a plot of land outside of the town's walls, east of its main gate, to Galway Corporation. Little would Mayor Eyre have thought that 300 years later this piece of ground would be such an important part of Galway life, let alone that it would still bear his family's name.

This book is not intended as a comprehensive study of Eyre Square, but rather to provide an insight into aspects of its history. The study draws from a wide range of archival, periodical, cartographical and visual sources. Extracts from contemporary accounts are interspersed throughout the text, which provide an interesting variety of opinion, positive and negative, about the Square.

The first part of the book deals with the early origins and development of Eyre Square, as it was gradually transformed from an extramural fair green to a landscaped town square. The second part of the book looks at its more recent history through its monuments. Whether visible or vanished, these 'ornaments' are testament to local and national cultural trends and political movements. The book concludes with a look at some of the various names, past and present, for the Square. It is my hope that this short book will kindle an interest in this historic and invaluable civic space.

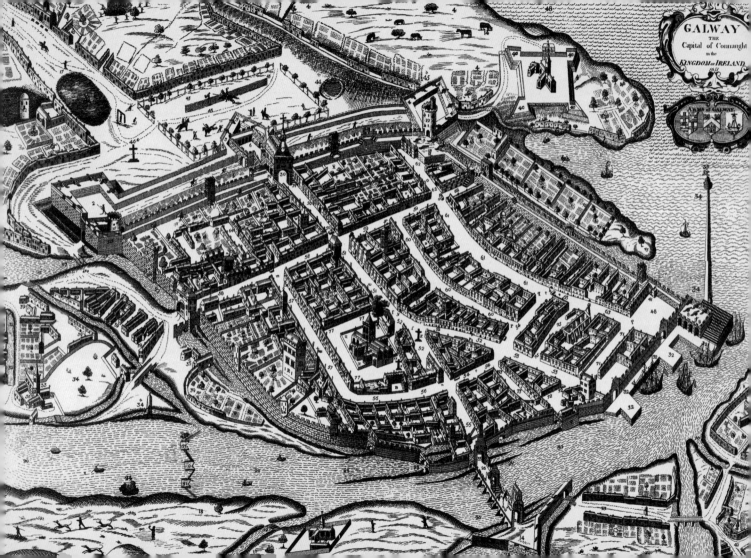

GALWAY THE Capital of Connaught in the KINGDOM of IRELAND 1651

ARMS of GALWAY

Origins and Development

Eyre Square is not, in fact, square. It is comprises of two parts; the southern area is rectangular in shape, and the northern one is roughly triangular. Although it is located in the heart of Galway today, for much of its history it was extramural, i.e. outside the town's walls. Over the centuries the square, which developed in tandem with the town, had a variety of purposes and was known by several names.

Left: Pictorial Map of Galway (1651) from Hardiman's *History of Galway* (1820). North is to the left of the illustration.

Origins

In the thirteenth century, the Anglo-Norman settlement of Galway developed around a castle built by the de Burghs. By the early fourteenth century, the town was enclosed by a curtain wall and was beginning to flourish as a result of trade. The town was compact and defensible. Its principal entrance, the Great Gate, faced eastwards, in front of which an open space was maintained: a defensive feature affording the town's defenders a field of fire in front of the main gate. Up until the early nineteenth century, this area was simply referred to as 'the Green'.

Tribes of Galway

A charter granted by King Richard III, in 1484, empowered Galwegians to elect their own mayor and bailiffs. It effectively released Galway from the grip of the de Burghs, and cleared the way for the rise to power of the 'Tribes of Galway'. A sustained period of prosperity followed under the leadership of these fourteen merchant families: Athy, Blake, Bodkin, Browne, D'Arcy, Deane, Ffont, Ffrench, Joyce, Kirwan, Lynch, Martin, Morris and Skerrett.

In 1630, Sir Valentine Blake (c. 1559-1634) of Menlo, Mayor of Galway, made the first attempt at landscaping this extramural plot: 'the square plot, at the green, outside the east gate ... was set apart for the purpose of public amusement and recreation; it was enclosed with wooden rails, and handsomely planted round with ash trees'.[1]

Pictorial Map

It would appear that none of the late fifteenth or early sixteenth century maps of Galway contain any details about the town's suburbs.[2] However, the mid-seventeenth century Pictorial Map of Galway shows the Green in detail for the first time. It depicts a rectangular plot, enclosed by railings, inside which there are twenty-nine trees visible. Within that plot, there are a number of men on horseback engaged in sport, with several onlookers. A footnote to the map, in Latin, translates as 'the green plots, where the gentry of the city solemnly (or on festive occasions) play, commonly called The Green'.[3] The map also depicts a gallows 'where justice is executed' and the 'New Market' indicated by a cross.[4] To the east and south of the Green there are a number of buildings. The two principal roads leading eastwards from the Green – 'the royal highway, otherwise the Great Lane, or *Bóthar Mór*' and 'the Little Lane (i.e. *Bóthar Beag)*' – are also lined with buildings;[5] the latter corresponds to the present Forster St. and College Rd.

The Eyres

The arrival of Cromwell's forces in 1651 heralded a long period of decline for Galway. After a nine-month siege, marked by famine and disease, the town finally surrendered. In the aftermath, Cromwell planted Galway with English settlers, many of whom had served with his army; one of

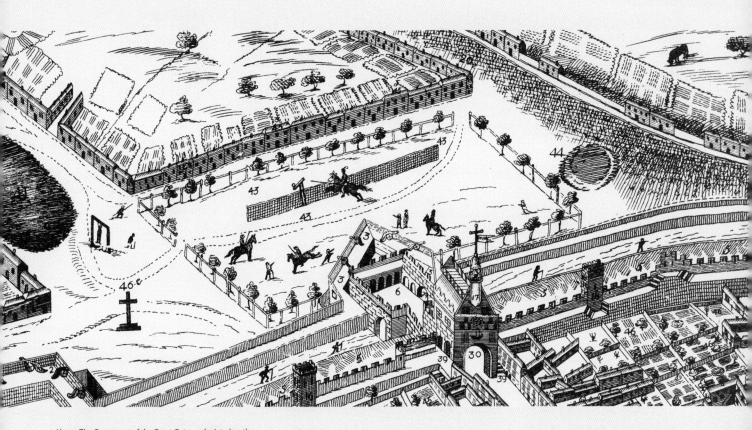

Above: The Green, east of the Great Gate, as depicted on the
Pictorial Map. North is to the left of the illustration.

these newcomers was Edward Eyre (1626-83). Eyre and his descendents became prominent figures in the affairs of the town. He was Recorder of Galway in 1659 and 1661, Mayor in 1663, and MP for Galway Borough between 1661 and 1666.[6] In 1670, Eyre acquired large tracts of corporation property, the majority of which lay outside the walls immediately east and south of the town, which included the Green.[7]

During the Jacobite-Williamite War (1688-91), Galway's fortifications were improved and extended to the east, infringing upon the Eyre properties. Despite these preparations, in July 1691, the town capitulated to General Ginkle and his Williamite forces. Subsequently, the Great Gate was replaced by a newer gate, which became known as Williamsgate.[8]

Eyre's son, Edward Eyre Jr. (1663-1739), a successful barrister, continued where his father left off, serving as MP for Galway in 1703 and Mayor between 1710 and 1712. During his time in office, he surrendered the ninety-nine year lease which his father had acquired from Galway Corporation, for more favourable terms. The corresponding entry in the Corporation Book of 12 May 1712 records: 'The necessity and advantage to the town and corporation, of having a spacious entrance open and unbuilt before William's-gate, leading to the east suburbs and to Boher-more, having been this day presented in council, alderman Edward Eyre (whose father, in 1670, obtained a lease of part of the said ground, with several other parcels,) declared

that he would agree to grant a piece of ground, containing about thirty perches, for that purpose; in consideration of which, the corporation, (himself being mayor), on the 19th of May following, extended the term of his lease for lives renewable for ever'.[9] Consequently, Saturday 12 May 2012, was celebrated as the official three-hundredth anniversary of 'Eyre Square', marking the date on which it was formally given to the town and its inhabitants.

Developments

The Green had long been a place for fairs and markets. In 1730, Galway Corporation obtained a patent for an additional weekly Monday market, four additional markets to be held on the four Friday preceding Christmas Day, together with three additional fairs (20 May, 10 September and 10 October) 'to be held on the square plot next the east gate of the town'.[10]

There was no notable expansion to the town for most of the eighteenth century, and the Green remained little changed. The closing decades of that century, however, witnessed the dawn of a period of economic growth and urban development. In his survey of Galway, Hely Dutton noted that at the time of the union 'the old useless wall was nearly demolished' and Galway 'began to flourish'.[11] It was at this time that the commercial and landed classes moved out of the medieval town to more salubrious accommodation built around the Green, and the poorer classes moved into the 'old town'.

In 1801, General Meyrick, who had been sent to Ireland during the disturbances of 1798, had a square of two acres enclosed with a low wall and laid out as a military parade ground. By the 1820s, the parade ground had become the 'principal walk for the beau monde' and 'a favorite promenade with the ladies'.[12]

Logan's Map of 1818, drawn for Hardiman's *History of Galway* (1820), depicts the developments which had taken place since the Act of Union. The walled square, at that time named after General Meyrick, was enclosed by roads on three of its sides, with a fourth 'new road' planned for its south side, constructed sometime between 1818 and the late 1830s. The terms 'Fair Green', 'Corn and Potatoe [sic] Market' and 'Hotels' feature at the northern end of Meyrick Square, indicating the variety of activity taking place.

From the 1820s onwards, Meyrick's Square became more commonly known as Eyre's or Eyre Square, after the Eyre family who had given the land to the town. However, it was not only its name that changed. The following decades would see dramatic developments that would transform and forever popularise the square.

Septem ornant montes Romam, septem ostia Nilum, Tot rutilis stellis splendet in axe Polus. Galvia, Polo Niloque bis æquas, Roma Conachtæ; Bis septem illustres, has colit illa tribus.

Rome boasts sev'n hills, the Nile its sev'n fold stream, Around the pole sev'n radiant planets gleam. Galway, Connacht's Rome, twice equals these; She boasts twice sev'n illustrious families.

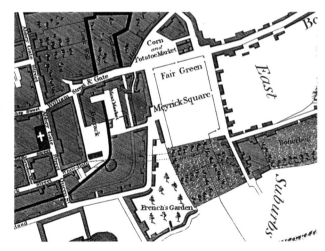

Logan's Map of Galway (1818).

1 Hardiman, 1820, 103.
2 Walsh, 2004, 274.
3 McErlean, 1905-6, 151.
4 McErlean, 1905-6, 151.
5 McErlean, 1905-6, 148.
6 Clavin, 2012, n.p.
7 Hayes McCoy, 1942-3, 58-9.
8 Walsh, 2004, 283.
9 Hardiman, 1820, 222.
10 Hardiman, 1820, 224.
11 Dutton, 1824, 197.
12 Dutton, 1824, 202 & Hardiman, 1820, 316.

From Fair Green to Town Square

From 1790 onwards Galway underwent something of a building boom, and the town began to expand beyond its medieval walls. This new phase saw the construction of Dominick St. on Galway's western fringes, and the erection of a great many new houses on the verges of the Green.[1] The town's population was also on the increase, growing by a third between 1813 and 1831, from 24,684 to 33,120.[2]

Postcard of a colour-tinted photograph from the Lawrence Studio (c. late 1800s). Courtesy of Philip O'Toole

Enclosing the Square

From the dawn of the new century, the Green became more enclosed as lofty buildings, both private and commercial, transformed the once open space into a Georgian town square. Hotels, such as the Claricarde Arms (1810) and the Royal Hotel (c. 1813), began to appear.[3] Some, such as the Clanricarde Arms, had posting establishments where travellers could hire post-horses, carriages and drivers to tour the surrounding districts. Banks, too, saw potential in the square and branches of the Provincial Bank (1826) and Bank of Ireland (1830) were built;[4] the National Bank moved to the square in the mid-1860s. From the late 1830s, the square was lit by gas lamps. The Galway County Club established a premises on the square (now Hibernian House), where the landed gentry met to discuss issues of mutual importance.

Despite these modern developments, agricultural markets and fairs continued to be held at the square. For the visiting tourist, the modern town square teeming with farmers and their animals was an incongruous sight. In later years, hiring fairs were also held at the square, at which spailpiní (seasonal farm workers) from Cois Fharraige and Connemara gathered to be hired by strong farmers from East Galway;[5] these continued to be held into the middle of the twentieth century.

A great, wide, blank, bleak, water-whipped square lies before the bedroom window; at the opposite side of which is to be seen the opposition hotel, looking even more bleak and cheerless than that over which Mr. Kilroy presides. Large dismal warehouses and private houses form three sides of the square; and in the midst is a bare pleasure-ground surrounded by a growth of gaunt iron-railings, the only plants seemingly in the place. Three triangular edifices that look somewhat like gibbets stand in the paved part of the square, but the victims that are consigned to their fate under these triangles are only potatoes, which are weighed there

Novelist, William Makepeace Thackeray, 1845.

GALWAY.

THE CLANRICARDE ARMS,

KILROY'S HOTEL,

EYRE SQUARE.

Is the best situated Hotel in Galway ; where the Tourist will find every comfort that can be sought for. Parties visiting Galway *en route* for

THE INTERESTING WILDS OF CONNEMARA,

will find this Hotel the most convenient, as it affords the necessary Comforts and Accommodation ; having in connexion

Mr. Bianconi's Coaches and Cars.

The following of which leave the Hotel daily :—

THE LIMERICK DAY COACH AND ROYAL MAIL CAR,

HEADFORT AND WESTPORT CAR,

TUAM AND SLIGO CAR,

OUGHTERARD AND CLIFDEN ROYAL MAIL COACH AND CAR.

Above: The Claricarde Arms & Bianconi's, Eyre Square (1854).

Above right: Lawrence photograph of tourist long cars & Bianconi coach, Eyre Square (c. late 1800s). Courtesy of the National Library of Ireland.

Stereograph of National Bank, Eyre Square (c.1870s). Courtesy of National Library of Ireland

Transportation

By the 1840s, Charles Bianconi's horse-drawn cars, known as 'Bians', connected provincial and market towns across Ireland including Galway, where his offices were located on the square, convenient to the hotels. The virtual monopoly that Bianconi held on the transport system was brought to an end with the arrival of the railways. In 1851, Dublin was linked with Galway by rail. The arrival of the railway and the subsequent construction of the Midland Great Western Railway (MGWR) Hotel did much to confirm Eyre Square's position as the town's main traveller hub.

While the town had much to attract travellers, including the Claddagh and Salthill, many used Galway as a gateway to 'the West'. Connemara, in particular, was much visited by Victorian tourists; the MGWR subsidised car services from Galway before the extension of the 'iron road' to Clifden (1895).[6]

In 1877, the Galway and Salthill Tramway Company was inaugurated, and two years later it opened a tramline linking its Forster St. depot, close to Galway Station, to its terminus at Salthill. The tramline ran along the south and west of Eyre Square, before turning onto Williamsgate St. and continuing its journey to the seaside resort, where its beaches and bath-houses had long since attracted visitors. The company eventually closed in 1919, as motorised transportation replaced horse-drawn transportation.

A Victorian Park

At the turn of the nineteenth century, the square, walled in by order of General Meyrick, was little more than a parade ground for the local garrison. By the 1820s, however, due to a lack of public walkways, it had become a popular place to promenade for the 'beau monde' and 'the ladies'. Although seen as sufficient in the absence of a better alternative, the square was not an ideal recreational space: it served as a fair green, and lacked the facilities associated with a town park typical of the period, such as railings, landscaping, and other ornamentation.

At that time, the square belonged to Robert Hedges Eyre (c. 1770-1840) of Macroom Castle, Co. Cork, who following the death of his elder brother, Edward, in 1803, succeeded to the Eyre properties in Galway. In 1836, Eyre offered to lease the square to the Galway Town Commissioners for public purposes, on the condition that it would be railed and maintained.[7] The Town Commissioners appointed a committee to deal with Eyre, through his agent Rev. James Payne. Following eighteen months of negotiations, a lease was signed, giving the square to the Town Commissioners at a nominal rent. The Eyre Square Committee immediately sought plans and estimates for the railing of the square[8] and, empowered by the Town Commissioners, set about collecting subscriptions to defray the expenses of railing in and planting the park.[9]

Swiftly we glide over the salt water estuary of Lough Athalia [sic], into the great terminus of Galway, at 1.45 o'clock, and out through it into the enormous limestone hotel, built, 'regardless of expense,' by the original directors of the railway; and from whence, after a 'bit and a sup,' we emerge among the beggars into Eyre-square, surrounded by hotels, club-houses, banks, private residences, and coach offices, whence the great 'Bian' can forward us to 'anywhere,' and in which we can choose our newspaper according to our politics or polemics Surgeon, William Robert Wills Wilde, 1867.

A red-haired tourist was sitting on 'the long car' in Eyre-square, Galway, awaiting its departure for Connemara. 'Throw me a penny, yer honnor,' said the beggar man. 'I will not,' replied the tourist, emphatically. 'Ah, thin,' retorted the vagrant, remembering how touchy red-haired people are to any allusion to their hair, 'maybe you'd leave me a lock to light my pipe with'. Belfast News-Letter, 3 Sept. 1898.

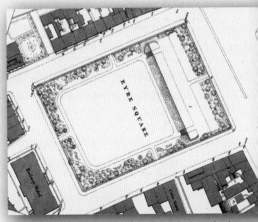

Above: O.S. Map of Eyre Square (1872) detailing the landscaped park.

The windows of the hotel (the only one in Galway) faced the market-place; and I could not help fancying the surprises which an Englishman would feel, if, without the immediate journey, he could be at once placed in the window of the hotel of Galway. The whole female population – congregated in hundreds – wore red jackets and red petticoats; and not a single pair of shoes and stockings were to be seen throughout the marketplace ... In every few pence laid out on potatoes (for potatoes were the only commodity at market), there were so many gestures, so much loud talking, and, apparently, such threatening attitudes, that one expected, every moment, to see the market-place converted into battle field. Travel writer, Henry David Inglis, 1838.

The Square the only place of recreation for the respectable portion of the public of Galway was, on Sunday last, thrown into such as scene of disorder that they were obliged to abandon it to the ferocious sport of a parcel of clowns, who were amusing themselves by letting a number of mastiffs loose upon an ill-fated badger. Not only did they annoy the poor brute in this manner, but they had the hardihood to levy pence and halfpence from every person who were so cruelly curios as to witness the sport. We understand it is intended to renew the exhibition on Sunday next again; and as we have no Magistrate in town who thinks it is his duty to put a stop to such rioting, we call upon the Church-wardens to interfere.

Galway Weekly Advertiser, 11 Feb. 1826.

(27) Eyre Square, Galway, centre of one of Ireland's famous old towns, rich in legends. COPYRIGHT 1903 BY THE AMERICAN STEREOSCOPIC CO.

Above: Stereograph of Eyre Square (c. 1903).

By August 1841, £500 of the estimated £800 needed to complete the improvement works had been contributed.[10] *The Galway Vindicator* reported that 'the stone plinth or dwarf-wall has been for some time finished and it is a capital piece of workmanship. It is proposed to erect on this a handsome iron railing and to lay out the enclosure tastefully with shrubs, flower-pots and walks – so that when finished it would rival the handsomest of the metropolitan squares'.[11]

In November 1841, John Fogarty, of Phoenix Ironworks, Limerick, was awarded the contract to rail the square. The appointment of Fogarty was not universally welcomed in Galway as for the majority the resident founder, Patrick Stephens, Merchants Rd., was the preferred choice. Although less experienced than Stephens, Fogarty's was, at £511, the lowest tender. He proposed to execute the work in wrought iron and committed to having the works completed by June 1842.[12] A fortnight later Fogarty met with the Town Commissioners 'with a model in wood of the upright bar, with the bottom ornament and spearhead, and portions of the upper and lower horizontal bars'.[13] In May 1842, there were proposals put before the Committee to introduce 'a spike four inches high between each of the bars with a view to prevent persons standing on the lower bar of the rail or dogs passing through'; the proposal was not resolved.[14]

With the railings completed, the Eyre Square Committee was given the task of considering and reporting on 'the regulations under which admission should be given to promenade in the square' and was unanimously of the opinion that 'it should be permitted to all decently clad people that chose to walk in it'.[15] The Committee resolved that 'on Sabbath and festival days the square be open to the public after divine service' and that keys be allowed 'to persons paying "2/6 for the key and 1/6 quarterly for the privilege such person to be responsible for the key'.[16] Subsequently, Fogarty was ordered to make sixty keys for the locks of Eyre Square.[17]

Despite the fact that the walkways and planting were not yet fully completed, the square was officially opened in August 1842. The military band of the 30th Depot, having obtained permission from the Town Commissioners, arranged to perform in the square every Monday and Thursday afternoon.[18] *The Galway Vindicator* reported that 'the Walks were crowded with the elite of Galway Society – Fashion and beauty delighted the eye, while the ear was charmed with the delicious harmony of the magnificent Band'.[19]

The new park was a great success and became a place for passive and active recreation. Galwegians picnicked on the grass and promenaded the circuit walkway, gossiped and listened to various bands; various sporting clubs – cricket, tennis, soccer – used the

Right: A Galway Mail Car (c. 1880s). Courtesy of National Library of Ireland.

A GALWAY MAIL CAR. 895. W.L.

Eyre Square Galway.

Above: Colour tinted postcard of Eyre Square. Courtesy of Philip O'Toole.

Eyre or Meyrick square, an oblong of about 180 yards by 130, is situated almost immediately east of the south-east limits of the ancient town and is edificed with good and lofty though plain buildings; but, in consequence of its interior area being enclosed by an ugly, dwarfish, gap-interrupted stone-wall, and unadorned with either lawn, or shrub, or statuary, and unqualifiedly abandoned to the melée of promenading, marketing, raree-show keeping, and children's gaming, it has a wan and almost rueful appearance... A somewhat triangular open area projects from the western half of the square, and is edificed on one side by the fine, large, head-hotel of the town, and on the other by buildings mixedly public and private, – good and indifferent.

Parliamentary Gazetteer of Ireland, 1846.

I had much pleasure in seeing, on Thursday last, an old friend with a new face. The Square of Galway once more assumes a gay and fashionable appearance, the military band attending on the occasion and, though the inanimate beauties of the Square be yet in embryo, still the assemblage of living beauty there left no want observable. It had long been a subject of complaint in Galway that it was deficient of a public walk to attract the gaily-disposed, to show off the belle, or to form a rally point where cheerful conversation might unite with healthful exercise. That want has now been happily supplied in the Square, and with unsparing trouble and attention, as the admirable and tasteful arrangements testify. Galway Vindicator, 6 Aug, 1842

grassy plot for both training and matches. Over the following decades, monuments and memorials were added and removed.

The railings remained a feature of Eyre Square for more than 120 years. In the winter of 1964, they were removed from the square in order to 'modernise' it and open it up to the surrounding streets. The decision was not a popular amongst Galwegians. In 1984, the railings were erected around the grounds of the Collegiate Church of St. Nicholas in place of its high surrounding wall.[20]

Meetings & Rallies

As Galway's largest open public space, Eyre Square became a natural focal point for all sorts of public meetings. Daniel 'the Liberator' O'Connell (1775-1847) and Charles Stewart Parnell (1846-1891) – two of the nineteenth century's most celebrated Irish orators – addressed large crowds in the square on the big issues of the day. In 1843, O'Connell came to Galway during his campaign for the repeal of the Act of Union.

The preparations for his visit, the culmination of which was a repeal dinner at Eyre Square, were unlike anything ever before seen in Galway and a pavilion, elegantly decked out and capable of accommodating six hundred people, was erected.

In October 1880, Parnell addressed a large and enthusiastic crowd of tenant farmers – many bearing banners with the motto 'the Land for the People' – from a platform erected at Eyre Square.[21] In February 1886, he spoke at the square in support of the election of Captain O'Shea in the Galway by-election of that year.[22] In the twentieth century, other historic figures followed the well-trodden path to Eyre Square, including Big Jim Larkin and John F. Kennedy.

Like many other town greens, Eyre Square was often used as a drilling and parade ground for the military. During the Great War (1914-18), it also became a focal point for British Army recruitment drives. The Royal Hotel, at the north of the square, became the recruitment premises for the Irish Guards Regiment when they were in Galway.[23]

In April 1915, at the invitation of the Urban District Council, the Irish Guards came to Galway. They were met at Galway Station by a vociferous crowd and a company of Connaught Rangers and John Redmond's National Volunteers. The following day, after attending morning mass at St. Nicholas' Old Pro-Cathedral, Middle St., the three regiments marched to Eyre Square and a meeting was held, resulting in the enlistment of forty men from the town.[24] During this period it was not unusual to see the Union Jack and Royal Standard flying at the square.

Above: Railings at Church Lane, Galway (2012)
Courtesy of Tanya Williams Photography.

Top Right: Eyre Square with railings (c. 1870-1910). Courtesy of National Library of Ireland.
Bottom right: Plaque commemorating re-erection of railings, Church Lane (2012). Courtesy of Tanya Williams Photography.

When news of the armistice reached Galway on 11 November 1918, the Connaught Rangers lit celebratory bonfires at Eyre Square[25]; four years later they were disbanded and marched through the square for the last time. In the aftermath of the war, veterans donning poppies marched to the square every first of July where they observed a two-minute silence in remembrance of their fallen comrades.[26]

By contrast, during the Second World War (1939-45) Eyre Square was a turf, rather than military, depot. Coal shortages from Britain meant that peat was in high demand in the capital. Thousands of tons harvested from bogs across Galway, were stacked in the square before being transported by road and rail to Dublin. To assist with 'The Emergency', *An Chéad Chath*, the Irish-speaking battalion of the Irish Army, stationed at Renmore Barracks, were engaged in turf-cutting.[27]

Green to Town Square

Between the late eighteenth and early twentieth century, the medieval green was developed into a Georgian/Victorian town square. During this time it became a multi-functional space: a place of trade and commerce, of sport and relaxation, of transport and tourism, and of conflict and celebration. Although the square was completely redeveloped in the mid-1960s, and again in the early 2000s, it has continued to provide Galway with an invaluable social and cultural space.

1 Dutton, 1824, 197.
2 Census of Population of Ireland, 1821 & 1831.
3 O'Dowd, 1985, 65 & MGWR, 1883, 133.
4 *Parliamentary Gazetteer of Ireland*, 1846, 244.
5 Connolly, 2004, 338.
6 Rowledge, 1995, 160.
7 Galway Town Commissioners' Minutes, 11 July 1836.
8 Galway Town Commissioners' Minutes, 18 Jan. 1838.
9 *Connaught Journal*, 2 April 1840.
10 *Galway Vindicator*, 21 Aug. 1841.
11 *Galway Vindicator*, 21 Aug. 1841.
12 *Galway Vindicator*, 4 Dec. 1841.
13 *Galway Vindicator*, 18 Dec. 1841.
14 Galway Town Commissioners' Minutes, 17 May 1838.
15 Galway Town Commissioners' Minutes, 3 Aug. 1842.
16 Galway Town Commissioners' Minutes, 3 Aug. 1842.
17 Galway Town Commissioners' Minutes, 11 Aug. 1842.
18 *Galway Vindicator*, 13 Aug. 1842.
19 *Galway Vindicator*, 20 Aug. 1842.
20 *Connacht Tribune*, 13 Jan. 1984.
21 *The Times*, 25 Oct. 1880.
22 *Glasgow Herald*, 11 Feb. 1886.
23 Henry, 2006, 32.
24 *Galway Express*, 1 May 1915.
25 Henry, 2006, 131.
26 Henry, 2006, 137.
27 Dáil Éireann Debate (Employment Schemes), 18 June 1942.

Above: Lawrence photograph of Galway & Salthill Co. tram, Eyre Square (c. 1880-1910). Courtesy of the National Library of Ireland.

The interior of the pavilion is neatly fitted up, and very liberally decorated with evergreens and festoons of flowers. From the centre pillars, which are covered with pink calico and wreathed with flowers, spring to either side of the pavilion four green triumphal arches, from which are hung the Galway arms, the bishop's arms, Lord French's arms, and the Irish harp. A decorated canopy overhands the chair, and above it will appear, in illuminated gas ... the crown between two stars, beneath it the shamrock placed between the Prince of Wales's initials, having on either side the Prince of Wales's plume and the Irish harp; and lower down, and much larger, the Royal initials. Over the main entrance, outside, are a crowd, the Royal initials, and the word 'Repeal' which will also be illuminated with gas. Lloyd's Weekly London Newspaper, 2 July 1843.

Galway Green, also called Eyre Square, is a very extensive area, surrounded by wide and handsome streets which contain some of the finest houses in the town. The centre or green is planted with trees and ornamental shrubs, and intersected with commodious and finely-gravelled walks, with convenient seats placed at different intervals, and surrounded with light and elegant railing. It is open from ten in the morning till an advanced hour in the evening, and is accessible to strangers, and to the inhabitants and their families who pay an annual sum of six shillings. In size and appearance it is equal to many, and superior to some, of the public squares in the principal cities. Travel Writer, Thomas Lacy, 1863.

MIDLAND GREAT WESTERN RAILWAY.

HOTEL

HOTEL

RAILWAY STATION. GALWAY. 888. W.L.

Railway Station & Hotel
(1851-52)

Surprisingly, in 1838, the Irish Railway Commission did not see the west of Ireland as a significant enough trade route to merit a railway line.[1] By 1845, however, the Midland Great Western Railway (MGWR) and the Great Southern and Western Railway (GSWR) were scrambling over each other in order to be the first to reach Galway, in the belief that its port – some 400 kilometres closer to New York than Liverpool – would become the main seaport for all transatlantic traffic between Europe and North America.

Left: Railway Station, Galway (c. 1877).
Courtesy of the National Library of Ireland.

MIDLAND GREAT WESTERN RAILWAY OF IRELAND.

OPEN TO GALWAY.

TIME and FARE TABLE for DECEMBER 15th, 1853.

Miles from Dublin	DOWN TRAINS. STATIONS.	Daily 7.0 Morn. 1,2,3 Class.	10.30 Morn. 1 & 2 Class.	4.0 Aftern. 1,2,3 Class.	5.0 Aftern. 1,2,3 Class.	MAIL 7.15 Even. 1 & 2 Class.	10.0 Night Goods &c.	Sunday 10.30 Morn. 1,2,3 Class.	MAIL 7.15 Even. 1,2 Class.	PASSENGERS 1st Class s. d.	2nd Class s. d.	3rd Class s. d.	4th Class s. d.	CARRIAGES Two wheels s. d.	Four wheels s. d.	HORSES One Horse s. d.	Two Horses s. d.	Three Horses s. d.
—	TRAINS LEAVE DUBLIN, at......	7.0	10.30	4.0	5.0	7.15	10.0	10.30	7.15									
4¼	Blanchardstown,......	....	*10.40	....	5.10	....	....	*10.40	....	0.10	0.8	0.6	0.5	—	—	—	—	—
7	Clonsilla,......	*7.20	10.50	*4.20	5.25	....	....	10.50	....	0.10	0.10	0.7	0.5	—	—	—	—	—
9	Lucan,......	....	*10.55	*4.25	*5.33	7.36	....	*10.55	7.36	1.8	1.0	0.9	0.6	—	—	—	—	—
11	Leixlip,......	....	*11.0	*4.32	5.40	7.42	....	*11.0	7.42	1.6	1.3	0.10	0.7	—	—	—	—	—
15	Maynooth,......	7.40	11.16	*4.42	5.54	7.52	10.45	11.16	7.52	2.6	2.0	1.3	0.10	5.0	9.0	5.0	9.6	13.6
19	Kilcock,......	7.50	11.25	*4.52	6.6	8.2	11.0	11.25	8.2	3.0	2.6	1.6	1.1	7.0	11.6	7.0	11.6	16.0
21	Ferns Lock,......	....	*11.30	4.58	....	....	....	*11.30	....	3.6	2.8	1.8	1.2	—	—	—	—	—
26½	ENFIELD,......	8.5	11.45	5.10	6.30	8.20	11.35	11.45	8.20	4.3	3.6	2.2	1.7	9.0	13.6	9.0	15.0	20.0
30½	Moyvalley,......	....	*11.55	*5.22	....	8.28	....	*11.55	....	4.8	4.0	2.6	1.10	—	—	—	—	—
36	Hill of Down,......	8.20	12.15	5.37	....	8.40	12.10	12.15	8.40	5.8	4.10	3.0	2.2	12.0	18.6	12.0	21.0	28.0
41½	Killucan,......	8.35	12.25	*5.55	....	8.52	12.35	12.30	8.52	6.3	5.8	3.3	2.7	14.0	21.0	14.0	24.0	32.6
50	MULLINGAR arrives at	....	12.50	....	....	9.15	....	12.52	9.15									
	leaves at	8.55	12.55	6.25	....	9.20	1.10	1.5	9.20	8.0	6.8	4.2	3.0	17.0	25.6	17.0	30.0	40.0
58	Castletown,......	9.15	1.15	6.50	....	9.38	1.40	1.25	9.38	9.0	7.6	4.10	3.4	19.6	30.0	19.6	35.0	49.0
62	Streamstown,......	....	*1.22	*7.0	....	....	2.0	*1.22	....	10.0	8.3	5.0	3.6	21.0	32.0	21.0	37.6	52.0
68	Moate,......	9.35	1.35	7.15	....	9.58	2.40	1.45	9.58	11.0	9.0	5.6	4.0	22.0	34.0	23.0	41.0	56.6
78	ATHLONE, arrives at	10.0	2.0	7.45	....	....	3.30	....	....									
	leaves at	10.20	2.10	....	....	10.22	....	2.15	10.22	12.6	10.6	6.0	4.0	26.0	39.0	26.0	47.6	64.0
91¼	Ballinasloe,......	10.55	2.40	....	....	11.5	6.55	2.45	11.5	15.0	12.0	7.0	4.6	31.0	46.6	31.0	55.6	74.6
101¼	Woodlawn,......	11.30	3.20	....	....	11.36	7.21	3.20	11.36	16.0	13.3	8.0	5.0	34.0	51.0	34.0	61.0	84.6
115½	Athenry,......	12.0	3.50	....	....	11.53	8.5	3.50	11.53	18.0	14.6	9.0	5.4	38.0	57.0	38.0	68.6	94.0
121	Oranmore,......	*12.20	*4.15	....	....	12.10	8.40	*4.15	12.10	19.0	15.3	9.6	5.9	40.0	60.0	40.6	73.6	100.0
126½	GALWAY,......	12.40	4.30	....	....	12.30 night	9.15	4.30	12.30 night	20.0	16.0	10.0	6.0	42.6	63.6	42.0	76.6	106.0
		P.M.	P.M.	P.M.	P.M.	night	A.M.	F.M.	night									

Midland Great Western Railway

Incorporated in 1845, MGWR was the third largest railway company in Ireland. In 1846, the company commenced its east-west line from Broadstone Station, Dublin. The Great Famine delayed proceedings but, in 1849, MGWR received a government loan of £500,000 to assist with the construction of the line, which they argued would relieve distress; by September 1850 there were 9,000 men employed on the works.[2] The railway contractor, William Dargan, completed the Athlone to Galway section before the specified contract time and the line between Dublin and Galway opened on 1 August 1851.[3] Contrary to the general expectation, the inauguration of the line was strictly a private affair.[4] The arrival of the railway brought an even greater focus to Eyre Square and encouraged the further development of hotel facilities in the vicinity.[5] It also revolutionised transport and tourism in the west. In the 1830s the mail coach from Dublin to Galway took sixteen hours; with the construction of the railway line the same journey took just five and a half hours by train.[6]

Galway Station

Galway Station was designed by the Dublin architect, John Skipton Mulvany (1813-1870), who built several stations throughout the 1840s, including Blackrock Station (1841), Dublin, and the new terminus at Kingstown, now Dún Laoghaire (1842). In 1845, Mulvany was appointed architect to MGWR and completed stations at Mullingar, Athlone and, in 1851, at Galway.[7] Richard Turner (c. 1798-1881), of Hammersmith Ironworks, Dublin, built the twenty-five metre span roof over Galway Station. It was the first design of its kind in Ireland and consisted of curved beams covered with corrugated iron, with a considerable glass centrepiece.[8] Turner also engineered the Palm House (1844-1848) at Kew, England, widely considered as the finest surviving Victorian iron and glass structure in the world.

In 1966, on the fiftieth anniversary of the 1916 Easter Rising, Galway Station was renamed Ceannt Station in memory of Éamonn Ceannt (1881-1916), the Galway-born signatory of the Proclamation of the Republic.

Railway Hotel

The thirteen-bay, four-storey MGWR Hotel (later the Great Southern Hotel, and now the Meyrick Hotel) was formally opened in August 1852. Mulvany and Dargan were responsible for the design and construction, which cost in the region of £30,000. Conveniently for travellers, Galway Station and the Railway Hotel, as it was known, were connected. Unlike the GSWR Railway Hotel at Killarney, Co. Kerry, which was run by the railway company, the MGWR Railway Hotel at Galway was instead leased to a series of managers.[9]

The Railway Hotel has since dominated the Eyre Square's southern skyline. It was hailed as 'the largest and most commodious provincial inn yet erected in the kingdom'[10] and was something of an unexpected surprise for visitors to the west: '[We] took up our quarters at the Railway Hotel, which far exceeded our expectations in the way of accommodation: we had no idea that there was such a capital house in that remote part of the country'.[11] The hotel was luxurious and affordable only to travellers of a certain class; indeed, such was the calibre of its guests that the local press listed the arrivals in its columns. It also became popular in 'fashionable circles' for its balls, which were regularly held and well attended.

The visit of one of the hotel's guests made national news. In 1857, Prince Louis Napoleon of France, having arrived in Galway aboard his yacht *La Reine Hortense*, stopped for lunch at the Railway Hotel before boarding a train for the midlands.[12] The visit sent shock waves through the British administration, ever fearful of French imperial expansion.

Galway Time

One of the many impacts of the railway was that it effectively ended 'Galway Time'. Galway, like other Irish towns, operated according to local time, which was relative to its distance from Greenwich, London. Being to the east, Greenwich time was earlier than Irish time. There was four minutes difference for every longitudinal degree west of the Greenwich meridian line, so Irish time was between twenty-five and forty minutes behind.[13]

The Railway Hotel at Galway is the largest that we saw in Ireland, and contains, as we had been informed, a "power o' beds" ... The inn forms one side of the principal Square, and the neighbour buildings being comparatively small and dingy, resembles some grand lady, in all her crinoline, teaching the third class at a Sunday school.

Dean of Rochester, Samuel Reynolds Hole [An Oxonian], 1859.

Top Left: New Line of Steam Ships to America (1859).

Bottom Left: Notice to Hotel Proprietors in *Railway Record* (1852).

Right: The MGWR Hotel (1859).

NEW LINE OF STEAM SHIPS TO AMERICA.

THROUGH FREIGHTS
From LONDON to NEW YORK (viâ Galway), calling at St. John's, Newfoundland, to land her Majesty's Mails and Passengers.

STEAM BETWEEN GALWAY AND NEW YORK,
THE SHORTEST AND MOST DIRECT ROUTE TO AMERICA.

Splendid and Powerful Ocean Mail Steam Ships will leave Galway for New York as under :—

To sail from Galway.	To sail from New York.
Circassian .... 25 June	Argo .. .. ——
Pacific .... ——	Prince Albert ...... ——
Adelaide .... ——	Circassian .... ——

MIDLAND GREAT WESTERN RAIL-WAY OF IRELAND.—Galway Hotel.— Notice to Hotel Proprietors.—The Directors are prepared to receive Proposals for Renting the above Hotel, which they are about to furnish throughout, exclusive of plate, linen, glass, &c. The Hotel is most eligibly situated, and will contain upwards of fifty bed rooms, with considerable accommodation as to reception rooms, and a spacious saloon or ball room, and will be ready for occupation by the 31st July next.

Proposals to be sent in on or before the 1st July, addressed to

HENRY BEAUSIRE, Secretary.
Dublin Terminus, 4th June, 1852.

THE MIDLAND
GREAT WESTERN RAILWAY HOTEL,

GALWAY.

This magnificent Hotel is unsurpassed, either in external appearance or internal arrangements, by any similar establishment in the kingdom, having been erected at an immense cost by the Directors of the Midland Great Western Railway for the special purposes of a hotel. It is beautifully situated, having the handsome pleasure-grounds of Eyre Square in front, and a view of the Bay in the rear; while internally it is provided with all the requirements needed for Comfort, as well as Luxury. Thorough ventilation having been a main object with the architect, corridors run the entire length of the building, and are lighted from domes in the roof; thus ensuring at all times a current of pure air, a want so frequently felt in similar establishments. On each floor are Hot, Cold, and Shower Baths, always ready. As the building forms the front of the Railway Terminus, visitors enter the Hotel from the platform, and thus avoid the annoyances attendant upon having to pass through the town. The Proprietor, J. DEANE, being extensively engaged in the wine trade, and importing his wines direct from the growers (and only those of the choicest vintages and most celebrated brands), is enabled to supply those who patronize his Establishment with the Choicest Wines at a reduced tariff, by saving for his customers all intermediate profits. Post horses, Cars, and Open Carriages attached to the Hotel, and to be had at a moment's notice, by application at the bar.

Great Southern Hotel, Galway.

Above: Postcard of Great Southern Hotel (c. 1930s). Author's Collection.

The change from Black's [Hotel] to the Railway [Hotel] was like one from barbarism to civilisation, and I found the latter hotel most clean, quiet, and comfortable, with a good dinner, and including herrings, no longer corned but fresh. On comparing, however, the bills of the two establishments I found Black's the more moderate of the two. Travel writer, William W. Barry, 1867.

Now there is a grand railway hotel, in which the service is performed not by a discalceated waitress, but by spruce waiters, smartly dressed after the Parisian and London fashion, in black clothing with white vests and cravats to match. You can have your linen washed and mangled, too, on the premises, not as speedily, indeed, as at New York, but quite as promptly as in London, Bath, or Brighton. Author, Andrew Valentine Kirwan, 1868.

In effect, Dublin time was twenty-five minutes behind London and Galway time was eleven and a half minutes behind Dublin. With the arrival of the railways, this became problematic for timetables as the local time at one end of the line could differ significantly from that at the other. As Irish trains operated to time in the metropolis – Dublin time – Galway had to conform.

Writing in 1868, Cusack Patrick Roney declared, incorrectly, that 'Dublin time has now become universal time in Ireland'.[14] Galway, however, was slow to adapt. In 1870, the Galway Express noted that Dublin time was the standard 'in every other town in Ireland'.[15] A few years later, the Galway town clock was synchronised with Dublin time, but in protest local publicans continued to serve drink beyond the official closing time.[16] 'Dillon's clock' on Williamsgate St., just off the square, reminded Galwegians that trains arrived and departed according to Dublin time and not local time.

The Definition of Time Act, 1880, legally standardised time in England and Scotland to Greenwich time and in Ireland to Dublin time. In 1916, Ireland officially adopted Greenwich Mean Time.

ARRIVALS AT THE RAILWAY HOTEL.

Captain Brown, 3rd Buffs; Mr. Ashworth and family; Lord Castlemain and Friend; Captain Coates, Captain Carlton and Lieutenant Wright, 3rd Dragoon Guards; Rev. Mr. and Mrs. Smith, Rev. Mr. Crozier, Captain Erving, and the Rev. Mr. Erving; Mr. and Mrs. Deacon, and the Misses Deacon; Captain Hawkins, Captain Frit and Friend; Dr. Thompson, Mr. Pitcairne and family, en route to Clifden; Rev. Mr. Frazer, Rev. Mr. Pierson, Mr. and Mrs. O'Leary, Mr. and Mrs. Blake, Mr. and Mrs. C. Mahon, Messrs. Gardiner, Leving, Knyvett, M'Credy, Leonard, Boyle, Davidson, Coddy, Douglas, Reigh, Moffatt, Moore, Ringwood, Lyle, and Mason, &c., &c.

THE EXCURSION TRAIN AND EMIGRATION.

Thirty-three persons proceeded to Dublin by the

1 Ferris, 2008, 23.
2 Ferris, 2008, 54-5.
3 Tatlow, 1920, 125.
4 *The Builder*, 16 Aug. 1851.
5 Walsh, 2004, 289.
6 Horner, 2007, 27.
7 Hourican, 2012, n.p.
8 Cowper, 1855, 265.
9 Rowledge, 1995, 154.
10 Fraser, 1854, 152.
11 Bulger, 1864, 227.
12 Collins, 1996, 137.
13 Dobbins, 2010, 180.
14 Roney, 1868, 111.
15 *Galway Express*, 8 Jan. 1870.
16 Cunningham, 2004, 167.

Left: Ceannt Station & Meyick Hotel (2012). Courtesy of Tanya Williams Photography.

Above Right: Arrivals at the Railway Hotel, *Galway Vindicator*, 6 July 1853.

40

RAILWAY HOTEL, GALWAY 771. W.L.

The Crimean Cannon
(1857)

After Britain's victory in the Crimean War (1853-56), towns and cities across Britain and Ireland were gifted captured ordnance as symbols of Imperial Britain's military might[1]. In 1857, Galway was gifted two Russian cannon by the Government's War Department for its loyalty and support during the war. The cannon were reputedly captured at the Battle of Inkerman in 1854, during which a significant amount of Russian ordnance fell into the hands of the 88th Regiment of Foot, later the Connaught Rangers. The Town Commissioners welcomed the tokens of appreciation and arranged a celebratory handing over ceremony.

Left: Crimean Cannon facing Railway Hotel (c. 1880-1910)
Courtesy of the National Library of Ireland.

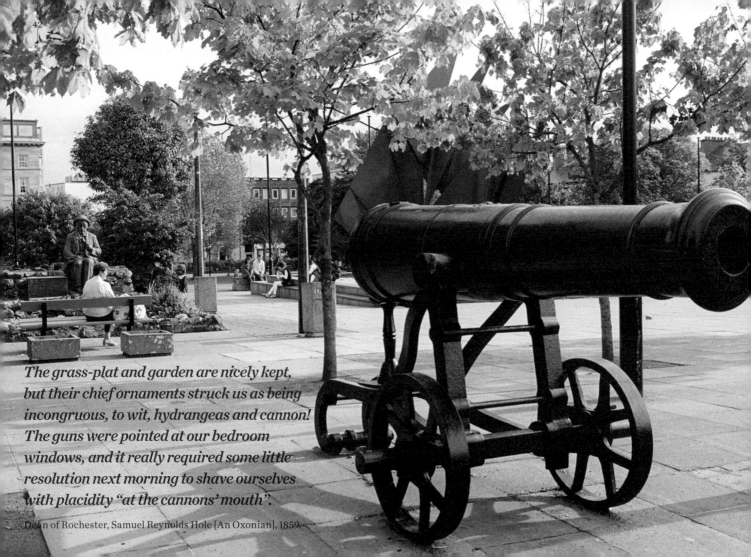

The grass-plat and garden are nicely kept,
but their chief ornaments struck us as being
incongruous, to wit, hydrangeas and cannon!
The guns were pointed at our bedroom
windows, and it really required some little
resolution next morning to shave ourselves
with placidity "at the cannons' mouth".

Dean of Rochester, Samuel Reynolds Hole [An Oxonian], 1859.

Under the headline 'The Sebastapol Trophies', the Galway Vindicator described in some detail how the pair of cannon was escorted from the Railway Terminus to Eyre Square by a procession, which included the High Sheriff and Town Commissioners, and was met by a large number of spectators – 'fashionable people of the town, businessmen and gentry from the county'[2]. Each weighing two tons, the cannon were placed in position upon the terrace, fronting the Railway Hotel and facing the square.

The Rev. Peter Daly, Chairman of the Town Commissioners, addressed the gathering saying that the cannon would 'remain as perpetual memorials of English and Irish valor'[3]. Soon after, the speeches were abandoned as a result of torrential rain but the festivities continued in the Town Hall, where select guests were treated to a 'dejeuner' with 'an abundance of champagne and other wines of choice and selected vintage' and musical entertainment provided by a German brass band.[4]

The toasts made on this occasion give an insight into the loyalties of the gathering. As per protocol, the first toast was to the health of Queen Victoria, then her consort Prince Albert, followed by the health of the Prince of Wales and the Lord Lieutenant. Each toast was received with polite applause and responded to 'appropriately'. When the rain had subsided, there was a fireworks display in Eyre Square after which the crowd returned to the Town Hall.

In the summer of 1858, Samuel Reynolds Hole, the horticulturist Dean of Rochester, made a tour of Ireland in the company of the illustrator John Leech. Writing under the pseudonym 'An Oxonian', Hole described the square and felt the cannon to be out of harmony with the flowery surrounds.

The cannon remained outside the Railway Hotel for several years until, in 1866, they were removed to Athlone Barracks by order of the authorities, which feared that the Fenians might attempt to re-service them and use them against the Crown. In 1867, William Wilde wrote that 'the Crimean guns, which had been pointed at the Railway Hotel in Eyre-Square, have been removed from the grasp of the "Irish Republic virtually established"'.[5] In 1868, following strong representations from the Town Commissioners, the cannon were returned to Galway; this time being placed on the upper terrace to the north of the square.[6] Apart from this brief absence, the Crimean Cannon were a feature of the square for almost 150 years, until they were moved to the grounds of City Hall, College Rd., during the Eyre Square Enhancement Project (2004-06).

1 Conway & Lambert, 2000, 53.
2 Collins, 1996, 138.
3 *Galway Vindicator*, 5 Aug. 1857.
4 *Galway Vindicator*, 5 Aug. 1857.
5 Wilde, 1867, 12-13.
6 Galway Town Commissioners' Minutes, 16 July 1868.

Left: Cannon at Eyre Square (1995). © RTÉ Stills Library.

Dunkellin Monument
(1873)

In 1867, William Wilde wrote that there was 'no public statue in the province of Connaught', apart from a white marble statue of King William III (erected in 1763), formerly situated on the bridge at Boyle, Co. Roscommon[1]. Wilde didn't have to wait long for another public statue. Following the death of Lord Dunkellin in the autumn of 1867, a memorial monument was commissioned; unveiled in 1873, it adorned the upper terrace of Eyre Square for almost half a century.

Left: Dunkellin Monument (c. 1873-90).
Courtesy of the National Library of Ireland.

What I complain of and what I think the people of Galway have reason to complain of, is this – that the only public square in Galway, and the only one which has been railed and planted by the people's money, should be sacrificed to pander to the ambition and to please the vanity of the friends of the deceased Lord Dunkellin. Is there any reason why the people of Galway should place Lord Dunkellin among the immortal gods, sacrifice their public square to honour him, and bow down their heads as they pass along the public streets in admiration of the late Lord Dunkellin. I answer emphatically – No! The Nation, 28 June 1873.

Lord Dunkellin

Ulick Canning de Burgh (1827-1867), Lord Dunkellin, was
the eldest son of Ulick John de Burgh (1802-1874), the first
Marquis of Clanricarde, a politician and wealthy land magnate
who lorded over one of the largest estates in Co. Galway. Born
in London, the Eton-educated Dunkellin pursued a military
career. In 1854, he fought in the Crimean War and was captured
at Sebastopol. He held the office of Member of Parliament
(Liberal) for Galway between 1857 and 1865 and for Co. Galway
between 1865 and 1867.[2] According to Roche, he was 'fairly
successful in the House of Commons, an excellent speaker and
a popular personality... he also showed capability in managing
the Clanricarde estates, and was popular with tenants'.[3] In 1867,
he died of Bright's disease (nephritis), a serious and at that time,
untreatable kidney disorder. His passing was mourned not only
by the Clanricarde family but also by many of his peers who saw
him as a favourable representative for their class.

Dunkellin Memorial Commitee

Soon after his death, several of his peers formed a memorial
committee in order to raise funds for a monument and oversee
its completion. A sum of £1,600 was raised within three months,
including £10 from the Prince of Wales (later George V).[4]
The committee resolutely decided that subscriptions for the
monument should be confined to Galway City and County, the
two constituencies Lord Dunkellin represented, and returned
several subscriptions received from outside the County. In
1873, the *Galway Vindicator* reported that the 'subscribers
included men of every shade of politics in the County and town
of Galway. Clergymen Catholic and protestant, noblemen and
gentlemen, professional and mercantile, all cordially united
in a determination to do honor to the memory of the late lord
Dunkellin'.[5] Almost fifty years later, the local press reported
conflictingly that it was 'subscribed for by the Clanricarde
tenantry, a good deal of which ... was obtained from the people by
threats'.[6]

John Henry Foley

The Committee agreed that the distinguished Anglo-Irish
sculptor, John Henry Foley (1818-74), should execute the work.
Although Foley was preoccupied with the O'Connell Monument
for Sackville St. (now O'Connell St.), Dublin, he accepted the
commission.

Foley's monument consisted of a 2.5m bronze statue of Lord
Dunkellin on top of a polished Peterhead red granite pedestal,
which stood on two steps of Aberdeen granite.[7] The politician
was depicted 'with arms folded, which he invariably assumed
when addressing a public'.[8] The inscription on the pedestal read:
'Lieu. Col. Lord Dunkellin, M.P., for the County of Galway. Born
1827. Died 1867. This statue was erected by the inhabitants of the
County and Town of Galway as a tribute of affection and respect

to his memory. 1873'. The memorial committee was impressed with Foley's work: 'in none of the great works, which have given him world-wide celebrity, has he shown more genius and skill than in the present instance, where, with only the slender assistance of a photograph, he has been enabled to produce the faithful likeness'.[9] The monument was placed at the northern end of the square, facing the Galway County Club and was flanked by the Crimean Cannons.

Unveiling

The unveiling ceremony took place in September 1873, during which the Town Commissioners formally accepted the monument from the Memorial Committee. The event 'gathered together most of the nobility and gentry of county, but of the people there seems to have been a scant attendance'.[10]

Hubert George de Burgh-Canning

As Lord Dunkellin predeceased his father, his younger brother, Hubert George de Burgh-Canning (1832-1916) inherited the family estate. The second Marquis of Clanricarde had little interest in Ireland or his estate and made a rare visit to Galway for his father's funeral. He also succeeded Lord Dunkellin as M.P. for Galway but, in 1871, resigned his seat in protest against the Land Act 1870, which was, he believed, 'fraught with injustice to the landlord'.[11]

In 1886, the Woodford evictions on the Clanricarde estate received worldwide attention and the estate became 'a symbol of landlord oppression'.[12] In September, a crowd assembled in Galway and led by a band marched to the County Gaol where they cheered for the Woodford prisoners and denounced Lord Clanricarde, the Chief Secretary and the Attorney-General for not allowing bail; they then continued to the Lord Dunkellin Monument, which they threatened to pull down or blow up using dynamite.[13]

In October, at a meeting of the Galway Town Commissioners one member submitted a notice of motion: 'that this Board remove the statue of Lord Dunkellin in the Square to some less prominent position more suitable to his character and the character of his successor the marquis of Clanricarde'.[14] The motion caused uproar, not least because the member in question cast aspirations on Lord Dunkellin's character; some of those who knew Lord Dunkellin personally were quick to come to his defence, whilst the chairman noted that 'a man's fault should die with him'.[15] When the furore was over, the motion was defeated by 7 votes to 12.[16]

Town Tenants League

Despite several threats from those opposing its presence in the square, the Dunkellin Monument survived in *situ* for almost half a century. In 1922, the bronze statue was pulled from its

Right: Dunkellin Monument & Crimean Cannons (c. 1904).
Courtesy of the National Library of Ireland.

EYRE SQUARE. GALWAY. 891 W.L.

pedestal by the Galway Branch of the Town Tenant's League, which sought similar entitlements for urban dwellers as had been conferred upon farmers by the land acts.[17] Speaking from the empty pedestal, S.J. Cremin, Secretary of the Transport Workers Union, said that the monument was 'a symbol of landlord tyranny, and they [the Town Tenant's League] intended to pull down every symbol of its kind in Ireland and put a monument of some good Irishman in its place'.[18] The statue was then dragged through the streets of Galway and given a mock funeral, before being dumped into the River Corrib, from whence it disappeared. In the aftermath of the incident, it was reported that 'armed Dáil and Executive forces' patrolled the streets of Galway.[19]

Mr Lynch failed to see what good Lord Dunkellin had done to this country to entitle him a statue in Galway. At the same time it was better to let it remain there in the cruel mockery of the position in which it is placed, with his back to the Russian cannons, from which it is said, he ran away. Galway Vindicator, 9 Oct. 1886.

Castlegar Memorial

The pedestal of the Lord Dunkellin Monument remained in Eyre Square throughout the 1920s and early 1930s. It was eventually incorporated into the Castlegar Civil War Memorial on the Tuam Rd., Galway.

1   Wilde, 1867, 13.
2   Cokayne et al, 2000, 238.
3   Roche, 1987, 26.
4   *Galway Vindicator*, 24 Sept. 1873 & Burdett, 1889, 354.
5   *Galway Vindicator*, 24 Sept. 1873.
6   *Galway Observer*, 27 May 1922.
7   Tuam Herald, 27 Sept. 1873.
8   *Galway Vindicator*, 24 Sept. 1873.
9   *Galway Vindicator*, 24 Sept. 1873.
10 *The Nation*, 27 Sept. 1873.
11 *House of Commons Debate (Irish Land Bill)*, 10 March 1870.
12 Conwell, 2003, 38.
13 *The Times*, 13 Sept. 1886.
14 Galway Town Commissioners' Minutes, 7 Oct. 1886.
15 *Galway Vindicator*, 9 Oct. 1886
16 Galway Town Commissioners' Minutes, 7 Oct. 1886.
17 Cunningham, 2004, 225.
18 *Galway Observer*, 27 May 1922.
19 *Galway Observer*, 3 June 1922.

I accept, then, with peculiar gratification, on behalf of the Municipality of Galway, the trust you have this day committed to our charge; and I earnestly hope that this statue may remain to future generations as a symbol of the social harmony which has ever happily existed amongst us, and as a testimony of our appreciation of Lord Dunkellin's high and sterling qualities of head and heart.

John Redington, Chairman of
Galway Town Commissioners, 1873.

Above Left: Valentine's postcard of
Dunkellin Monument (c. 1909).
Author's Collection.

Right: Postcard of 'Ancient Doorway'
showing empty pedestal (c. 1930).
Author's Collection.

BROWNE'S ARCHWAY, GALWAY

Browne Doorway
(1905)

The 'Browne Doorway' is the name given to the seventeenth century arched doorway and oriel first floor window, originally belonging to the house of Galway merchant Martin Browne. Beneath the window, an armorial stone dated 1627, bears the names and family arms of Martin Browne and his wife Marie Lynch; both families belonging to the Tribes of Galway. The doorway stood on Lower Abbeygate St. which, when the house was built, was known as Skinner's St. or Glover's St.[1]

Left: Postcard of 'Browne's Archway' (c. 1950s).
Author's Collection.

The doorway is a fine example of Renaissance craftsmanship which shows that Galway, at that time, was more under continental than English artistic influence: a reflection of the close contacts between the town and the Continent as a result of trade.[2] During the nineteenth century, many travel writers visiting Galway remarked on the Spanish appearance of the town and, indeed, of its people.[3]

In the late nineteenth century, the doorway and window were salvaged from the ruins of Browne's house before it was demolished; the stonework lay in neglected condition for some time afterwards and some of its fragments were lost.[4] In 1905, following proposals from the Galway Archaeological and Historical Society, Galway Urban District Council and County Council erected the Browne Doorway as the northern entrance to a railed Eyre Square.[5] Since the removal of the railings in 1964 the doorway has stood as a lone sentinel.

The Browne Doorway was due to be relocated to Galway City Museum but, in 2002, *An Bord Pleanála* ruled that the 'Browne's Doorway shall be retained in its current location in the Square or relocated within the Square' because 'it is considered that the removal of the Doorway would be injurious to the cultural heritage of the Square'. Since the ruling, a transparent protective case has been erected around the lower portion of the doorway.

Part of the house built in the year of our Lord 1627 for Martin Browne, merchant, was removed from ruins in Lower Abbeygate Street and was erected here in 1905, to witness to the architectural character of the great houses that were built in the days of Galway's civic opulence.

Browne Doorway plaque

1   Hardiman, 1820, 28.

2   O'Sullivan, 1983, 449.

3   See, for example, Inglis, 1838, 212 & Rodenburg, 1886, 246-7 &

4   Anon., 1904-05, 64.

5   Anon., 1904-05, 63-64.

Left: Simmons of Galway photograph of the Browne Doorway, Abbeygate St. (c. 1890s).

Above: Browne Doorway (2012). Courtesy of Tanya Williams Photography.

Ó Conaire Monument
(1935)

Born in a house by the docks in Galway in 1882, Patrick Joseph Conroy (Pádraic Ó Conaire) lead an unconventional and relatively short life. Orphaned before his teenage years, he was raised by relations in Connemara and Co. Clare. He was educated at Blackrock College, Dublin, in the company of a young Éamon de Valera, before immigrating to London. By day Conroy worked for the British civil service and by night Ó Conaire taught Irish language classes with the Gaelic League. Encouraged by his fellow Leaguers, he began to write short stories, for which he won several literary awards.

Left: Ó Conaire Monument, Eyre Square (1974).
© RTÉ Stills Library.

PADRAIC O' CONAIRE MEMORIAL, GALWAY.

The Irish people of his generation owe it to themselves, no less than to him, to show their appreciation of his genius by placing a stone over his grave, or by founding a worthy memorial in his honour. With this objective a committee has been formed, with headquarters in his native town, where his body lies, and this committee now appeals to all those who hold our language and literature in esteem to associate themselves with this project by sending us a contribution, great or small. Gaelic League memorial subscription card

Influenced by the works of the great French, German and Russian writers, Ó Conaire was not afraid to tackle serious or taboo issues and was both lauded and castigated by his contemporaries. Following his return to Ireland in 1914, he earned a meagre living from teaching and writing, spending much of his time in Co. Galway. His later years were characterised by poverty, ill-health and alcohol abuse. In 1928, at the age of 46, he died in the pauper's ward of Richmond Hospital, Dublin, and was buried in his hometown of Galway.

Albert Power

Soon after Ó Conaire's death, his friends in the Galway Branch of the Gaelic League decided to erect a memorial in his honour and a subscription card was issued in order to raise funds. By the end of 1930, £200 had been secured towards the memorial.[1]

The Gaelic League recruited the services of master-sculptor, Albert Power (1881-1945), to execute the work. Born in Dublin, Power trained at the Dublin Metropolitan School of Art during the Celtic Revival. Following Independence, he was in high demand as a sculptor of nationalist memorials for the Irish Free State.

Far Left: Pádraic Ó Conaire (c. 1920s). Courtesy of Tom Kenny.

Top Left: Postcard of the Ó Conaire Monument, Eyre Square (c. 1940). Author's Collection.

Bottom Left: Sean Phádraic, Eyre Square (c. 1966). Courtesy of Galway City Museum.

Power initially proposed to seat a statue of Ó Conaire on the plinth formerly occupied by Lord Dunkellin, empty since 1922. He later spurned this idea, stating that it would have been 'grotesque, bizarre, altogether absurd'.[2] Instead the monument saw a statue of Ó Conaire seated on a stone wall in a naturalistic setting. Unusually, rather than idealising the writer, Power chose to depict Ó Conaire as he was remembered in his later years: unkempt and ravaged by excessive drinking.

Unveiling

In June 1935, the Ó Conaire Monument was unveiled in Eyre Square by Éamon de Valera and was well received. The ceremony, conducted through Irish, was broadcast on national radio. De Valera's speech focussed on the Irish language, reflecting the government's preoccupation with re-establishing the language as Ireland's *lingua franca* and Galway's important role in becoming 'not alone the first city of the Gaeltacht but of the whole of Irish-Ireland'.[3]

The monument became a place of pilgrimage for those who knew Ó Conaire, his works and for Irish language enthusiasts. It was also popular with tourists and over the following decades it became an iconic image of Galway, and one of its best-loved and most photographed landmarks.

Moving Statues

In the mid-1960s, Galway Corporation received funding from Bord Fáilte Éireann, as part of its resorts scheme, to help develop and modernise Eyre Square. The Eyre Square Improvement Scheme, as it became known, entailed the removal of the iron railings from around the square in order to make the park more spacious and to open it up to the surrounding streets.

As part of this modernisation, the statue of Ó Conaire was removed from its original setting and location and placed on the periphery of the square. Many Galwegians reacted angrily and the statue was eventually located more centrally, and without the naturalistic setting designed by Power.

The new situation left the statue more exposed to the public. A local newspaper reported that 'a favourite holiday pose is for Pádraic to be photographed with a lady with her arms around his neck – KISSING HIM'; one angry councillor remarked that 'taking photographs beside the statue is not so bad, but when holidaymakers start smudging it with lipstick, that is making a hare out of it altogether'.[4]

Right: De Valera unveiling the Ó Conaire Monument, Eyre Square (1935). Courtesy of Galway City Museum.

	2			5
1		4	
	3		

1: Shane Hunt with Sean Phádraic (1946). Courtesy of Shane Hunt.

2: The Naughton family from Rosmuc, Connemara (c. 1966). Courtesy of Michael Naughton.

3: Maureen Finnegan seated on Sean Phádraic's lap (1969). Courtesy of Maureen Finnegan.

4: Pat Moynihan from Co. Kerry (1935). Courtesy of Eleanor Hough.

5: Mary Conneely (left) with Sean Phádraic (c. 1970). Courtesy of Mary Conneely.

I actually counted fifteen cattle grazing there [Eyre Square] – the most expensive bit of grazing this side of Brussels. As if to add insult to injury we have the Ó Conaire Monument which is like a magnet to the hundreds of children between the ages of five and seventy-five who sprawl all over this very fine piece of Irish sculpture, posing for the camera. I doubt very much if the O'Connell Monument in Dublin, the Fr. Mathew statue in Cork or the Treaty Stone in Limerick are subjected to the same abuse as the Ó Conaire monument in Galway.

Councillor J. F. King, *Galway Advertiser*, 23 Jan. 1975.

I am furious that someone would even think of removing him from the Square. Phádraig is the one memory left of the Square, and if he goes then there is no Square as far as I'm concerned.

Letter to the Editor, *Galway Advertiser*, 29 May 2003.

I won my way through the crowd-guarded gate of Eyre Square and went in. A short walk on the gravelled path and I was before the man I had come so far to see. There was a great peace about him as he sat there, leg crossed upon leg, hat rakish on his head, mute in the sculptured dignity of stone. And around him were songless birds and the brown timidity rabbit. Sean Phádraig Ó Conaire.

Writer, Sigerson Clifford, *Irish Press*, 4 Feb. 1937

66

Ó MAOILÍOSA

Liam Mellows Monument
(1957)

In August 1957, the Catholic Bishop of Galway,
Dr. Browne unveiled and blessed a memorial statue
at Eyre Square to Liam Mellows (Liam Ó Maoilíosa),
the revolutionary who had led an insurrection in
Co. Galway during the 1916 Easter Rising.

Left: Mellows Monument, Eyre Square (2012).
Courtesy of Tanya Williams Photography.

Liam Mellows

Liam Mellows (1892-1922) was born in Lancashire, England, but raised from a young age in Co. Wexford and, subsequently, Co. Cork. In 1912, he was sworn into the Irish Republican Brotherhood and was later appointed its representative to the Irish Volunteers. When the Volunteers fractured in 1914, Mellows was sent to rebuild the organisation in Co. Galway.[1] He led the Galway insurrection in Easter 1916, and two years later was elected as a Sinn Féin candidate for the constituencies of East Galway and Meath.

An opponent of the Anglo-Irish Treaty, Mellows was captured during the Irish Civil War and interned in Mountjoy Jail. On 8 December 1922, he was executed by firing squad, along with three other senior anti-Treaty prisoners, as a 'reprisal' by the Provisional Government of the Irish Free State.

Domhnall Ó Murchadha

In 1952, on the thirtieth anniversary of the execution of Mellows, the Cork-born sculptor, Domhnall Ó Murchadha (1914-1991) was commissioned to complete a monument to the republican. Largely known for his church commissions, Ó Murchadha created a number of works in the 1950s and early 1960s honouring casualties of the War of Independence and Civil War.[2] The work, which took two years to complete, comprised a limestone figure of Mellows in military uniform, on top of a block ashlar limestone pedestal. According to the *Connacht Tribune*, the Co. Galwaymen's Association of New York subscribed $1,590.35 (£393/8/0) towards the completion of the work.[3]

A monument to Edward 'Ned' Lyons, at Newport, Co. Mayo, unveiled in 1962, is very similar in character to that of Mellows. Ó Murchadha's work can also be seen at Galway Cathedral: three tympana reliefs in Portland stone over the main entrance depicting baptism, confirmation and ordination.[4]

It is for his great qualities as a man and a soldier that his comrades keep him in abiding memory and that they have erected this statue to him. One of the most remarkable and significant facts is that even those who differed from him when the division caused by the Treaty came in 1922 have joined in erecting this statue. The death of Liam Mellows was one of the greatest tragedies of the Civil War.

Bishop Browne of Galway, *Irish Independent*, 19 Aug. 1957.

Inscriptions

As well as naming the sculptor and the architect (Diarmuid Ó Tuathail), the pedestal of the statue bears a number of inscriptions (in Irish): *I ndíl-chuimhne ar Liam Ó Maoilíosa ceann-phort Óglach Chondae na Gaillimhe san Éirigh Amach Seachtmhain na Cásga 1916* ('In memory of Liam Mellows leader of the Co. Galway Volunteers in the 1916 Easter Rising'); *Siad a chomrádaithe féin agus a lucht leanamhna in Éirinn agus i Nua-Eabhrach a thóg an leacht cuimhneacháin seo ina onóir* ('This monument is erected in his honour by his comrades in Ireland and New York'); and *A Mhuire gan small guidh air chun Dé* ('Virgin Mary pray to God for him').

Unveiling

On the day of the unveiling a special mass was held at St. Nicholas' Pro-Cathedral, after which the Tulla Pipers' Band from Co. Clare led a parade of IRA ex-servicemen through the main streets of Galway to the memorial site. The unveiling was attended by the sculptor, representatives of Galway Co. Council and Galway Corporation, as well as friends and relatives of Mellows.

1   Coleman & Murphy, 2012, n.p.
2   Turpin, 2003, 75 & 77.
3   *Connacht Tribune*, 3 Aug. 1957.
4   Turpin, 2003, 75.

Right: Carved inscription on Mellows Monument (2012).
Courtesy of Tanya Williams Photography.

Kennedy Memorial
(1965)

*In June 1963, President John F. Kennedy (1917-1963)
undertook a four-day visit to Ireland. Kennedy's eight
great-grandparents had emigrated from Ireland to Boston
in the mid-nineteenth century and, as President of the
United States, he embodied the emigrant success story.*

Left: President Kennedy at Eyre Square (1963).
Courtesy of the *Connacht Tribune*.

72

On 29 June 1963, President Kennedy visited Galway and was made a Freeman at a ceremony in Eyre Square, after which he delivered a short, emotionally charged speech before an enthusiastic crowd. Before departing the Square, he remarked: 'I must say that though other days may not be so bright as we look toward the future, the brightest days will continue to be those in which we have visited you here in Ireland ... you send us home covered with gifts, which we can barely carry, but most of all you send us home with the warmest memories of you and your country'. Five months later, after a mere 1,000 days in office, President Kennedy was assassinated in Dallas, Texas.

In June 1965, it was announced that the park at Eyre Square would be renamed the John F. Kennedy Memorial Park and that a limestone monument to the late president would be erected.[1] In August, Cardinal Richard Cushing of Boston (1895-1970), in the presence of President Éamon de Valera and Taoiseach Seán Lemass, dedicated and blessed the park and unveiled the memorial monument.

The memorial monument, a limestone wall, 2m high and 3m wide, had as its centrepiece a bronze profile of President Kennedy, which was cast from a bas-relief wood carving by local artist Albert O'Toole.[2] An inscription in English and Irish read: 'John Fitzgerald Kennedy, President U.S.A., became a Freeman of Galway Borough, at this place on June 29th, 1963'.

If the day was clear enough, and if you went down to the bay, and you looked West, and you sight was good enough, you would see Boston, Massachusetts. And if you did, you would see working on the docks there some Doughertys and Flahertys and Ryans and cousins of yours who have gone to Boston and made good. I wonder if you could perhaps let me know many of you here have a relative in America who you would admit to if you would hold up your hand? I don't know that it is about you that causes me to think that nearly everybody in Boston comes from Galway.

U.S. president, John F. Kennedy, 1963

[Kennedy] loved the outdoor life and the exquisite beauties of nature... this Park, dedicated to his memory, is a fitting memorial to him. May it inspire all of Galway, especially the young, to seek the higher things in life.

Cardinal Cushing of Boston, *Connacht Tribune*, 21. Aug. 1965

Cardinal Cushing, the son of Irish emigrants, was a life-long friend of the Kennedy family. On the same day as the unveiling of the Kennedy Memorial, Cardinal Cushing dedicated Galway Cathedral – Our Lady Assumed into Heaven and St. Nicholas – in which there is a wall mosaic of President Kennedy. In 1975, the Kennedy Monument collapsed and was removed; it was subsequently redesigned and re-erected. It was relocated to the east of the park during the Eyre Square Enhancement Project (2004-06).

1   *Connacht Tribune*, 26 Jun. 1965.

2   *Connacht Tribune*, 26 Jun. 1965 & Cathal & Sullivan, 2003, 36.

Above Left: Kennedy Memorial, Eyre Square (1960s). Above right: Bronze profile of President Kennedy (2012). Courtesy of Tanya Williams Photography.

Quincentennial Fountain
(1984)

In 15 December 1484, Richard III of England (1452-1485) granted Galway a charter of incorporation. In doing this, the king 'confirmed all former grants, and renewed the powers to levy the tolls and customs, which he directed should be applied towards the murage and pavage of the town; he also granted licence that they might, yearly, for ever, choose one mayor and two bailiffs'.[1] The charter essentially wrested Galway from the grip of the de Burgos, who had controlled the settlement since its foundation. It also paved the way for the subsequent dominance of the fourteen Tribes of Galway.

Left: The Fountain at Night.
Courtesy of Discover Ireland West.

To commemorate the five-hundredth (or quincentennial) anniversary of this momentous occasion, Galway Corporation commissioned a fountain for Eyre Square, which was sponsored by the regional branch of the Bank of Ireland. The official unveiling took place on the 15 December 1984 and was the culmination of a yearlong celebration in Galway.

An open competition for the design of the fountain was won by the Derry-born, Dublin-based architect, Eamonn O'Doherty (1939-2011). His entry, entitled *Claddagh Sails*, envisaged a 10m high structure in weathering steel, based on the form and colour of the sails of the traditional workboat of Galway Bay: the hooker. The fountain has since become one of Galway's most recognisable landmarks.

O'Doherty is today best-known for his large-scale outdoor sculptures, which include the *Anna Livia Fountain* (O'Connell St., Dublin, 1988; since relocated to the Croppy Acre Memorial Park, Dublin), *Crann an Oír* (Central Bank Plaza, Dublin, 1991), *Skellig* (Caherciveen, Co. Kerry, 1995), and the *Great Hunger Memorial* (Westchester, New York, 2001).[2]

The judges were unanimous in awarding first place to O'Doherty, commenting that his design 'answered in quite dramatic fashion the problems posed of strength of image, unifying power and symbolism in a Galway context ... it is also a most successful fusion of modern technology and traditional form. The assessors feel that this conclusion to the competition will provide Galway with a unique and distinctive commemorative sculptural fountain in its quincentennial year'.[3]

In describing the design, O'Doherty suggested that: 'the fountain symbolises the foundation and growth of Galway based on sea trade and its location astride the Corrib linking East Galway and Connemara ... the topmost part suggests the sails of ships at harbour against the rising buildings of the growing town. The sculpture in cor-ten steel will weather to a red-brown colour'.[4] In 1989, following another open competition, Galway Corporation commissioned O'Doherty to create a sculpture for the grounds of City Hall; entitled *The Corrib*, the limestone piece depicts a salmon leaping.[5]

1   Hardiman, 1820, 69.
2   Lynch, 2008, 85-7.
3   *Connacht Sentinel*, 10 Jan. 1984.
4   *Connacht Sentinel*, 10 Jan. 1984.
5   Hill, 1998, 220.

Left & right: Quincentennial Fountain (2012). Courtesy of Tanya Williams Photography.

An Faiċe Móṙ
EYRE SQUARE

Barḋas na Gaillime

Square Names

The place now known as Eyre Square had many names over the centuries. Some of these names coexisted, so that neighbours living on the square sometimes used different addresses, whilst other names never attained widespread popularity.

Left: An Fhaiche Mhór, Eyre Square (2012).
Courtesy of Tanya Williams Photography.

The Green

The earliest maps of the city, that bother to name the area, refer to the open plot as the Green (sometimes with an extra 'e', as in Greene), or the Fair Green, and this is how it was commonly referred to up until the early nineteenth century.

Meyrick Square

From about 1801, it became known as Meyrick's or Meyrick Square, after the military governor of Galway, who had walled in a rectangular portion of the green. General Meyrick had been sent to Ireland during the Rebellion of 1798, where he served until 1802, having command at Clonmel, and subsequently at Galway.[1] Whilst in Galway, Meyrick was responsible for instigating several developments in the town, including the Fish Market at the Spanish Arch.[2] It is referred to as Meyrick Square on Logan's Map (1818).

Eyre Square

From about 1820 onwards the square became more commonly known as Eyre's or Eyre Square, after the Eyre dynasty. At the time of the renaming, Robert Hedges Eyre, of Macroom Castle, Co. Cork, had inherited the Eyre properties in Galway.3 Robert Hedges Eyre died without issue – childless – in 1840 and was succeeded by his grandnephew, the Rev. Robert Hedges Maunsell Eyre. In 1852, the Eyre's Galway properties were sold

in the Incumbered Estates Court, thus ending the Eyre family's two-hundred-year association with the square.[4] It is referred to as Eyre Square on the first O.S. Map for Galway (1842).

Parnell Square

From the 1880s onwards, with Irish nationalism on the rise, many local authorities began nationalising the old names of bridges, streets and squares under their jurisdiction, particularly those with a colonial connection, often renaming them after Parnell and O'Connell.[5] In December 1899, some members of the Galway Urban Council formed a committee whose task it was to propose alternative names for Galway's streets.[6] The committee suggested renaming Eyre Square in honour of Charles Stewart Parnell (1846-1891). There were also recommendations with regards to some of the streets around the square – Williamsgate and William's St. to be Dillon St.; Shop St. to be O'Connell St.; Eglinton St. to be Wolfe Tone St.; Eyre St. to be Lord Edward St.; Victoria St. to be O'Neill Place and Forster St. to be St. Patrick's St.[7] The patriotic proposals were eventually defeated by a vote of six to four.[8]

Fr. Griffin Square

In May 1922, the Galway Branch of the Town Tenants League met in the square and proclaimed to the assembled masses that it was now to be called Father Griffin Square[9] after Fr. Michael Griffin (1892-1920), a local priest and republican sympathiser, who had been abducted and murdered by Crown Forces two years earlier. Although the curate was a popular figure, the name never caught on.

John F. Kennedy Memorial Park

In 1965, two years after the visit of American President, John F. Kennedy, to Galway, the recreational space – the grassy area and paved terrace – within the square was officially named the John F. Kennedy Memorial Park. Confusingly, the streets surrounding the park retained the name Eyre Square. Galwegians rarely, if ever, use the name John F. Kennedy Memorial Park, preferring instead to refer to the whole square as Eyre Square.

An Fhaiche Mhór

In Irish, the square has long been known as *An Fhaiche Mhór*, or *An Fhaithche Mhór*, meaning 'great green' or 'great lawn', and is still referred to as such by Irish speakers today. The Irish word faiche also appears elsewhere in the city: *An Fhaiche Bheag* ('small green') and *An Fhaiche Fhada* ('long green').[10]

1 Urban, 1830, 87.
2 Hardiman, 1820, 308-9.
3 Hayes McCoy, 1942-3, 157.
4 Hayes McCoy, 1942-3, 69.
5 Alter, 1974, 117.
6 Galway Urban District Council Minutes, 7 Dec. 1899.
7 *Galway Observer*, 30 Dec. 1899.
8 *Galway Observer*, 6 Jan. 1900.
9 *Connacht Tribune*, 3 June 1922.
10 Ó Maille, 1946, 48.

Right: New Names for Galway Streets, *Galway Observer*, 30 Dec. 1899.

NEW NAMES FOR GALWAY STREETS.

A Committee of the Galway Urban Council, consisting of Messrs E J Lee, Francis Lydon, Andrew O'Connor, R J Cooke, and Nicholas Lydon, met on Monday week in connection with the re-naming of the streets. After considerable discussion the following list of recommended changes was drawn up, and will be submitted to the next general meeting of the Council :—

Eyre Square	to be	Parnell Square
Williamsgate St. and Wm street	,,	Dillon street
Shop street	,,	O'Connell street
Mainguard street	,,	Emmett street
Bridge street	,,	O'Brien street
Wm street West and Sea Road	,,	Washington street
Lombard street	,,	St. Nicholas street
Churchyard street	,,	Foster Place
Middle street	,,	St. Bridget street
High street	,,	Sarsfield street
Eglinton street	,,	Wolfe Tone street
Eyre street	,,	Lord Edward street
Victoria street	,,	O'Neill Place
Street from corner of Town Courthouse to Corrib Terrace	,,	Tara street
Wood Quay	,,	Aughrim street
Henry street	,,	Burke street
Forster and College street	,,	St Patrick street
Newtownsmith	,,	McMahon street
New Line	,,	Moore street
Newcastle Road	,,	Davis street
Mill street	,,	St Joseph street
Market street	,,	John McHale street
Abbeygate street	,,	Grattan street Upr. and Grattan street Lower
Poor House Lane	,,	Vincent street.

RAILWAY HOTEL GALWAY. 4224. W.L.

Bibliography

Left: Crowd at Eyre Square (c. 1880-1910).
Courtesy of the National Library of Ireland.

Primary Sources

Census of Population of Ireland, 1821 & 1831 [online source].

Dáil Éireann Debate (Employment Schemes), 18 June 1942 [online source].

House of Commons Debate (Irish Land Bill), 10 March 1870 [online source].

Minute Books of Galway Town Commissioners Minutes, 1836-1899 [Hardiman Library, NUI, Galway].

Minute Books of Galway Urban District Council, 1899-1922 [Hardiman Library, NUI, Galway].

Secondary Sources

ANON. (1904-05) 'Proceedings, Notes, etc.' *Journal of the Galway Archaeological & Historical Society*, Vol. 4, pp. 63-64.

ANON. (1846) *The Parliamentary Gazetteer of Ireland, 1844-45* [PGI]. Vol 2. Dublin: A Fullarton & Co.

ALTER, P. (1974) 'Symbols of Irish Nationalism'. *Studia Hibernica*, No. 14, pp. 104-123.

BARRY, William Whittaker (1867) *A Walking Tour Round Ireland in 1865, by an Englishman*. London: Richard Bentley.

BULGER, George Ernest (1864) *Leaves, from the records of St. Hubert's Club: or Reminiscences of Sporting Expeditions in Many Lands*. London: L. Booth.

BURDETT, Henry Charles (1889) *Prince, Princess, & People*. Longman's, Green & Co. London.

BUTTERFIELD, Peter & McELROY, Martin (2012) 'Bianconi, Charles'. *Dictionary of Irish Biography*. Cambridge University Press & Royal Irish Academy [online edition].

CATHAL, Liam & SULLIVAN, Edmund (2003) *Forever Green: Ireland Now & Again*. Cincinnati, OH: St. Padraic Press.

CLAVIN, Terry (2012) 'Eyre, Edward'. *Dictionary of Irish Biography*. Cambridge University Press & Royal Irish Academy [online edition].

COKAYNE, G.E., GIBBS, V, DOUBLEDAY, H.A, WHITE, G.H., WARRAND, D. & DE WALDEN, H. (eds.) (2000) *Complete Peerage of England, Scotland, Ireland, Great Britain & the United Kingdom, Extant, Extinct or Dormant, Vol. 3*. Gloucester: Alan Sutton Publishing.

COLEMAN, Marie & MURPHY, William (2012) 'Mellows, William Joseph ('Liam')'. *Dictionary of Irish Biography*. Cambridge University Press & Royal Irish Academy [online edition].

COLLINS, Timothy (1996) 'The Town Hall in 1857: When Galway Hospitality Met Crimean Cannon'. *Journal of the Galway Archaeological & Historical Society*, Vol. 48, pp. 137-42.

CONNOLLY, Michael C. (ed.) (2004) *They Change Their Sky: The Irish in Maine*. Orono, ME: University of Maine Press.

CONWAY, H. & LAMBERT, D. (2000) 'Buildings & Monuments'. In: WOUDSTRA, J. & FIELDHOUSE, K. (eds.) *The Regeneration of Public Parks*. London & New York, NY: E&FN Spon. pp. 45-58.

CONWELL, J.J. (2003) *A Galway Landlord During the Great Famine: Ulick Burgh, first marquis of Clanricarde*. Dublin & Cork: Four Courts Press.

COWPER, E.A. et al (1855) 'Discussion: Description of the iron roof, in one span, over the joint railway station, New Street, Birmingham'. *Minutes of Proceedings of the Institution of Civil Engineers*, Vol. 14, pp. 264-72.

CUNNINGHAM, John (2004) *'A town tormented by the sea': Galway, 1790-1914*. Dublin: Geography Publications.

DOBBINS, Gregory (2010) *Lazy Idle Schemers: Irish Modernism & the Cultural Politics of Idleness*. Dublin: Field Day Publications.

DUTTON, Hely (1824) *A Statistical & Agricultural Survey of the County of Galway*. Dublin: Royal Dublin Society.

FERRIS, Tom (2008) *Irish Railways: A New History*. Dublin: Gill & Macmillan.

FRASER, J. (1859) *Handbook for Ireland*. Sackville St, Dublin: William Curry & Co.

FRASER, J. (1854) *A Handbook for Travellers in Ireland*. Dublin: James McGlashan.

GEOGHEGAN, Patrick M. (2012) 'Eyre, Robert Hedges'. *Dictionary of Irish Biography*. Cambridge University Press & Royal Irish Academy [online edition].

GWYNN, S.L. (2006) 'Canning, Hubert George de Burgh, second marquess of Clanricarde (1832-1916)'. In MAUME, Rev. Patrick (ed.) *Oxford Dictionary of National Biography*, Oxford: Oxford University Press [online edition].

HARDIMAN, James (1820) *History of the Town & County of the Town of Galway*. Dublin: W. Folds & Sons.

HAYES McCOY, Marguerite (1942-3) 'The Eyre Documents in University College, Galway'. *Journal of the Galway Archaeological & Historical Society*, Vol. 20, pp. 57-74 & pp. 151-79.

HENRY, William (2006) *Galway & the Great War*. Cork: Mercier Press.

HILL, Judith (1998) *Irish Public Sculpture: A History*. Dublin: Four Courts Press.

HORNER, Arnold (2007) 'Ireland's time-space revolution: improvements to pre-Famine travel'. *History Ireland*, Vol. 15, No. 5, pp. 22-27.

HOURICAN, Bridget (2012) 'Mulvany, John Skipton'. *Dictionary of Irish Biography.* Cambridge University Press & Royal Irish Academy [online edition].

INGLIS, H.D. (1838) *A Journey throughout Ireland during the spring, summer & autumn of 1834.* Vol. II. London: Whittaker & Co. [5th ediction].

KIRWAN, A.V. (1868) 'A Fortnight in Ireland in the Lent of 1863'. In: *Fraser's Magazine, Fishing Excerpts, Vol. 4 (1861-8).* London, pp. 670-83.

LACY, Thomas (1863) *Sights & Scenes in our Fatherland.* London: Simpkin, Marshall & Co.

LEWIS, Samuel (1837) *A Topographical Dictionary of Ireland, comprising the several counties, cities, boroughs, corporate, market, & post towns, parishes, & villages, with historical & statistical descriptions.* London.

LYNCH, Brian (2008) 'Eamonn O'Doherty: Genius Loci'. *Irish Arts Review*, Vol. 25, No. 1, pp. 84-87.

McERLEAN, J. (1905-6) 'Notes on the Pictorial Map of Galway (continued): The Index to the Map' *Journal of the Galway Archaeological & Historical Society*, Vol. 4, No. 3, pp. 133-60.

McDOWELL, R.B. (2009)'Burgh, Ulick John de, first marquess of Clanricarde (1802-1874)'. In MATTHEW, Rev. H. C. G. (ed.) *Oxford Dictionary of National Biography.* Oxford: Oxford University Press [online edition].

MGWR (1883) *Descriptive Guide to the Midland Great Western Railway: Dublin to Galway & the West of Ireland.* Dublin.

MINCH, Rebecca (2012) 'Foley, John Henry'. *Dictionary of Irish Biography.* Cambridge University Press & Royal Irish Academy [online edition].

MURPHY, William (2012) 'Griffin, Michael Joseph'. *Dictionary of Irish Biography. Cambridge University Press & Royal Irish Academy [online edition].*

MURRAY, John (1864) *Handbook for Travellers in Ireland.* London: John Murray.

O'DOWD, Peadar (1985) *Old & New Galway.* Galway: Archaeological, Historical & Folklore Society.

Ó MÁILLE, T.S. (1946) 'Áit-ainmneacha i gCathair na Gaillimhe' *Journal of the Galway Archaeological & Historical Society*, Vol. 22, pp. 43-48.

O'SULLIVAN, M.D. (1983) *Old Galway.* Galway: Kenny's.

OXONIAN, An [HOLE, S.R.](1859) *A Little Tour in Ireland.* London: Bradbury & Evans.

PIGOT, J. (1824) *Provincial Directory of Ireland.* London: J. Pigot & Co.

ROCHE, D. (1987) 'Later Clanricardes'. In: Woodford Heritage Group, *Clanricarde Country.* Galway: Connacht Tribune, pp. 17-29.

RODENBERG, Julius (1866) *Island of the Saints.* London: Chapman & Hall.

RONEY, Cusack Patrick (1868) *Rambles on Railways.* London: Effingham Wilson.

RONEY, Cusack Patrick (1866) *How to Spend a Month in Ireland.* Dublin & London: W. H. Smith & Sons.

ROWLEDGE, J.W.P. (1995) *A Regional History of the Railways of Great Britain: Ireland, Vol.* 16. Penryn, Cornwall: Atlantic Transport Publishers.

SLATER, Isaac (1846) *Slater's National Commercial Directory of Ireland.* Manchester: Slater.

SOMERVILLE, Edith (1893) *Through Connemara in a Governess Cart.* London: W. H. Allen & Co.

TATLOW, Joseph (1920) *Fifty Years of Railway Life in England, Scotland & Ireland.* London: The Railway Gazette.

THACKERAY, William Makepeace (1845) *The Irish Sketchbook of 1842.* London: Chapman & Hall.

TURPIN, John (2003) 'Domhnall Ó Murchadha: Sculptor with a Gaelic Vision'. *New Hibernia Review*, Vol. 7, No. 3, pp. 71-79.

URBAN, Sylvanus (1830) *The Gentleman's Magazine & Historical Chronicle, from July to December, 1830, Vol. 100, Pt. 2.* London: J.B. Nichols & Son.

WALSH, Paul (2004) 'Galway: A Summary History'. In: FIZPATRICK, Elizabeth, O'BRIEN, Madeline, & WALSH, Paul (eds.) *Archaeological Investigations in Galway City, 1987-1998.* Bray, Co. Wicklow: Wordwell, pp. 269-91.

WILDE, William Robert (1867) *Lough Corrib, its Shores & Islands: with Notices of Lough Mask.* Dublin: McGlashan & Gill / London: Longmans, Green & Co.

WILLIAMS, Jeremy (2012) 'Turner, Richard'. *Dictionary of Irish Biography.* Cambridge University Press & Royal Irish Academy [online edition].

Newspapers & Periodicals

Belfast Newsletter
The Builder
Connacht Tribune
Connacht Sentinel
Connaught Journal
Galway Advertiser
Galway Express
Galway Observer
Galway Vindicator
Galway Weekly Advertiser

Glasgow Herald
Irish Independent
Irish Press
Irish Times
Lloyd's Weekly London Newspaper
Railway Record
The Nation
The Times
Tuam Herald

86

Acknowledgements

Much of the research for this book was undertaken in preparation for an MA dissertation (on Albert Power's statue of Pádraic Ó Conaire) for University of Ulster. In consequence, thanks are due to those who helped with the initial research, as well as to those who have helped bring this book to fruition.

Thanks to Jim Higgins, Heritage Officer, Galway City Council; Patria McWalter, Maureen Moran and Petrina Mee at Galway County Library; Kieran Hoare, Margaret Hughes and staff at Hardiman Library, NUIG; Ciara Kerrigan and Keith Murphy at National Library of Ireland; Nora Thornton at National Photographic Archive, and Pearl Quinn at RTÉ Stills Library.

I am indebted to the following for providing photographs: Mary Conneely; Maureen Finnegan; Teresa Gilmore; Jimmy Higgins; Eleanor Hough; Shane Hunt; Mattie Hynes; Tom Kenny; Aengus McMahon; Michael Naughton and Philip O'Toole.

A big thanks to Tanya Williams (and Ross Molloy) for the beautiful contemporary shots (and a fun day out).

I am particularly grateful to John Burke and Lorna Elms whose keen eyes and valuable suggestions made all the difference to the final draft.

Special thanks to Niall McNelis for his enthusiastic support of this project from the onset; to Breandán Ó hEaghra for his advice and encouragement; to Ronnie O'Gorman for kindly agreeing to write the foreword, and to Cian O'Broin, Meyrick Hotel, for his generous sponsorship.

A big thank you to the ever-cheerful and much-talented Barry Jordan, Spear Design.

Above all, an extra-special thanks to my ever-patient wife, Vicky.

Left: The Raindrops showband with Sean Phádraic (c. 1970). Courtesy of the Jimmy Higgins.

EYRE SQUARE GALWAY. 774. W.L.

Above: View of Eyre Square from the Railway
Hotel. Courtesy of National Library of Ireland.

Right: Eyre Square from Richardson's Corner
(2012). Courtesy of Tanya Williams Photography.